Love you

Cell

Uncle Jim
&
Aunt Alice

D1710289

Mississippi Rescue

I. A. Garner

ISBN 978-1-64559-228-0 (Paperback)
ISBN 978-1-64559-229-7 (Hardcover)
ISBN 978-1-64559-230-3 (Digital)

Covenant Books, Inc.
11661 Hwy 707
Murrells Inlet, SC 29576
www.covenantbooks.com

Mississippi
Rescue

Elizabeth Ann Garner

One day, while traveling on the Mississippi River, something wonderful happened. It was a very rainy day. There were lots of objects floating in the river. My friends and coworkers were traveling on a tugboat, pushing barges of coal down the Mississippi River to Baton Rouge, Louisiana. The coal will be loaded on a ship that is traveling to China. There had been so much rain that the river was flooded with basketballs, coolers, lawn chairs, and a porch deck. Debris was floating everywhere. Anything that was on the banks of the river was washed away by the force of the flood.

The barges are maintained by deckhands. Deckhands are men and sometimes women that walk out on the barges and check

the tow, making sure the cables are tied and holding the barges together. Deckhands, along with boat captains and pilots, play a big part in river safety. The captain of the boat steers the tugboat, along with help from their pilots, while pushing the barges down the river. Maybe one day you could go to the river and see a riverboat working. Throw up a wave, and the nice captain will toot the horn for you in return. Tugboats move so much more product on the river for less cost than semitrucks or trains can on dry land. The cost is less because of the buoyancy of the river. Now that you know what a deckhand does, you understand they are always looking and listening to make sure every barge and every person is safe.

One day while checking tow, the deck crew heard the sound of a baby crying. They were frantic, wondering what it could be. The weather was stormy and very dangerous. After walking up and down thirty barges, there it was crying like a real baby. It was trapped between two barges that were side by side. The water was gushing all over the deckhands. They were brave and very determined to free whatever this was drowning. They managed to adjust the barges, and there it was, a tiny baby beaver. It was crying for its life, almost drowned by the swift and forceful water. It was a lucky day for the baby beaver and the whole crew on the boat. This little fella brought us much joy. We were so thankful for the rescue. On this shift there was a crew member named Nate, one named Brody, and there was Coleman, Luke, Aiden, and Cameron. There were six men working on this shift while six other deckhands were sleeping. Once their shift was over, the other crew members would work while they slept. Crew members are always on watch to work and keep everyone all safe as we travel the river moving the product to its destination.

Now back to our newfound friend. The little beaver was so frightened of the water, he just shook. Nate wrapped him in a towel to dry him off. He was very afraid, shivering and shaking while crying for his family of which he had been displaced. Nate held him in the towel and rubbed the top of his little head very gently. We were all looking on and hoping to soothe and comfort the little fella.

Brody said, "We have work and research to do, and we must come up with a care plan. I don't know anything about beavers. Do any of you?"

We all looked at each other. "No, we don't!" stated the rest of us.

As the cook, my name is Kamrie, I searched the Internet to plan the little beaver a diet. Luke researched the habits of beavers.

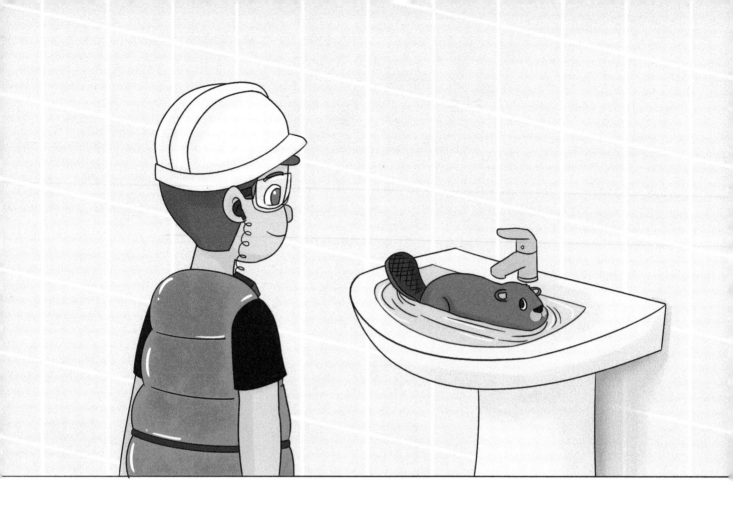

Coleman came up with a great plan. He thought the little beaver should swim in Aiden's bathroom sink. This would surely help him get over his fear of water. Each deckhand has a room with a tiny closet and bed and a small bathroom. Oh wow, there was so much we needed to do for the little fella.

9

Aiden found a large box and put rags and sticks in it. Nate put the little beaver in the box. He immediately started building and playing with the sticks and rags. He would stack them up in one corner of the box, then tear it down and move it to another corner! All day, every day, he worked so hard, nonstop doing this until he was tired! He would look up at Nate and slap his little tail until he picked him up.

The little beaver was fond of all the crew, but he had a special bond with Nate. I know he must miss his mother and beaver family. We are all his family now. Ha, ha, ha, I am sure we looked pretty different to this little one. Meanwhile, I discovered that beavers are vegetarians, so I fed the little one spinach, lettuce, and carrots. He was adjusting to his new family. He would even take a swim in Aiden's bathroom sink now. We were all so happy that he had overcome his fear of water and was enjoying swimming.

Coleman spoke up. "We must give the little beaver a name."

Once again, we all looked at one another.

Brody said, "Well, we don't know if it's a boy or a girl."

Coleman said, "I know, we will call it Mississippi. If we find out it's a girl, we will call her Miss Mississippi."

Aiden chimed in, "That is a great idea since we found the little one on the Mississippi River."

We did not tell the captain at first because we are not supposed to have animals on the boat. He came down from the wheelhouse (where he steers the boat), and there was Mississippi in the box. Nate told him of the rescue, and he asked the captain to let us take Mississippi to Baton Rouge, Louisiana, to a conservation officer. This would help ensure that Mississippi would have a good home. They would know what was best for our sweet, entertaining, spoiled little friend. The captain agreed.

It was the best trip on the river we had ever had. Mississippi was so much fun slapping his tail to attract his audience. In reading, we learned that beavers never leave their families. They work together to make a home and live as a family. Our little friend I am sure missed his family, just being two weeks old. It was a blessing to the baby beaver and to us to become its family. We were able to show it love, help it adjust, and overcome its fear of swimming. The water was so high and dangerous, I don't think Mississippi would have survived.

Thanks to a tugboat crew that did its job well and searched for whatever was crying, Mississippi was rescued, cared for, and placed in a good home. We safely and caringly handed little Mississippi to the conservation officer named Mollie Kate. Mollie Kate ensured us the Louisiana Conservation Department would take good care of our little friend.

About the Author

Elizabeth Ann Garner is a great-grandmother, who retired from the great state of Tennessee. She has written many true stories of real-life experiences. Some hilarious about her grandchildren, also many heartwarming stories of great courage and faith. Writing has always been her passion. She has faced adversity many times in her life and always persevered. This book was birthed from a very different road she had to travel after retirement. This is one more interesting true story from this season of her life. Some of the characters are named after her great-grandchildren. They were her inspiration for sharing this story. The great-grandchildren loved to hear stories of their Nanny's adventures on the river. She sincerely hopes her audience will enjoy it also.

CPSIA information can be obtained
at www.ICGtesting.com
Printed in the USA
LVHW070453090120
642993LV00001B/1/P